CITIES AT WAR

AMSTERDAM

★ ★ ★

Victoria Sherrow

New York

Maxwell Macmillan Canada
Toronto

Maxwell Macmillan International
New York Oxford Singapore Sydney

FOR MY FATHER-IN-LAW, SANDOR KAROCZKAI, WITH LOVE

All photos courtesy of the Rijksinstituut voor Oorlogsdocumentatie, Amsterdam. Special thanks to the researchers for their help in identifying photos and supplying background information on Amsterdam during the war years.

New Discovery Books
Macmillan Publishing Company
866 Third Avenue
New York, NY 10022

Maxwell Macmillan Canada, Inc.
1200 Eglinton Avenue East
Suite 200
Don Mills, Ontario M3C 3N1

Macmillan Publishing Company is part of the Maxwell Communication Group of Companies.

First Edition

Printed in the United States of America

10 9 8 7 6 5 4 3 2 1

Library of Congress Cataloging-in-Publication Data
Sherrow, Victoria.
        Amsterdam / by Victoria Sherrow.
                p.   cm. — (Cities at War)
        Includes bibliographical references.
        Summary: A brief account of Dutch history precedes a description, including many firsthand observations, of the German occupation of Amsterdam from 1940 to 1945.
        ISBN 0-02-782465-9
        1. World War, 1939-1945—Netherlands—Amsterdam—Juvenile literature. 2. Amsterdam (Netherlands)—History—Juvenile literature. [1. World War, 1939-1945—Netherlands. 2. Amsterdam (Netherlands)—History.] I. Title. II. Series.
D802.N42A457 1992
940.53'492353—dc20   91-31627

CONTENTS

★ ★ ★

A frozen canal makes a speedy thoroughfare for skaters during the winter of 1939-1940.

★ ★ ★ ★ ★ ★ ★ ★ ★

1

A PEACE-LOVING PEOPLE

The winter of 1939-1940 brought icy weather to the Netherlands. In the capital city, Amsterdam, people wore heavy woolen clothing as they took streetcars, taxis, boats, or bicycles to go to work, do errands, or attend school. Children skated along Amsterdam's frozen canals. At home, Amsterdammers warmed themselves in coal-heated rooms and ate thick pea soup, a traditional winter meal. Life in the city seemed as peaceful and orderly as usual, but the Dutch were uneasy. They listened closely to their radios, waiting for the latest news about World War II, which had afflicted Europe since the previous year.

A neutral country, Holland was surrounded by nations at war. It shared an eastern border with Germany, which since 1933 was a dictatorship under the control of Adolf Hitler and his Nazi party. To the west, across the North Sea, was Great Britain. When Nazi troops invaded Poland in 1939, Poland's allies, Britain and

France, declared war on Germany. By 1940, Nazi Germany included Austria, and its military troops occupied Czechoslovakia and Poland. Dutch leaders complained that their small country was "caught between the devil and the deep sea." Located by the North Sea, the people of Amsterdam feared that they would be engulfed in the ever-widening war.

Amsterdam had long battled both foreign invaders and the sea. One-fifth of Holland is located below sea level, so for centuries the Dutch had worked to turn swampland into cities, towns, and farms. During its history, Holland also had often been occupied by more powerful nations. The Romans conquered the region in 12 B.C. In the 700s, the Frankish emperor, Charlemagne, took control, making Christianity the official religion. Holland and Belgium were united and were called the Low Countries.

A series of German and French feudal lords ruled in Amsterdam until the Low Countries became part of the Hapsburg Empire, centered in Austria-Hungary, in the early 1500s. In 1543, the Spanish King Charles V was named their ruler. Conflicts arose because some people living in the Low Countries had rejected the official Catholic religion to become Protestants. During the 1500s, thousands of Dutch people were killed for their religious beliefs during a series of trials known as the Spanish Inquisition.

From 1568 until 1648, Dutch soldiers fought against Spain for their independence, led by William of Orange, a German-born Prince who owned estates in Holland. During this famous Eighty Years War, Amsterdammers contributed manpower and ships to win important victories at sea. But 19 years after defeating Spain, Holland had to fight again, to defeat the French. Another peaceful period ended when Napoleon Bonaparte conquered Holland in 1810.

In 1815, when Napoleon was defeated at Waterloo, Belgium,

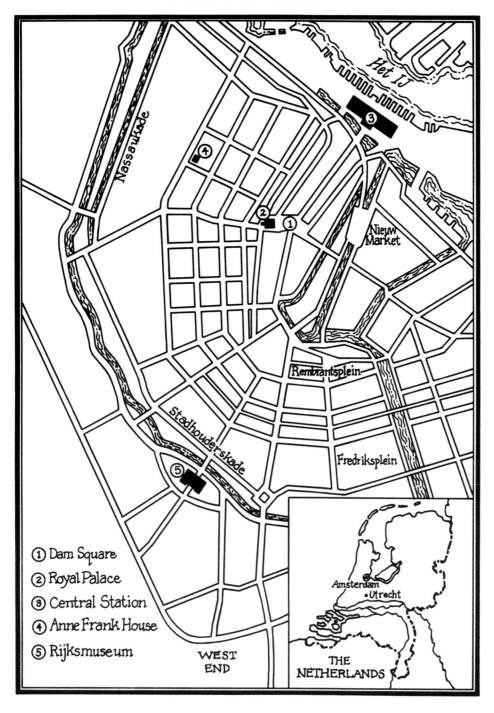

1 Dam Square
2 Royal Palace
3 Central Station
4 Anne Frank House
5 Rijksmuseum

WEST END

THE NETHERLANDS

by combined troops from England, Russia, and Prussia, the Low Countries again became free. Holland became the Kingdom of the Netherlands, with a written constitution and parliamentary monarchy. Under this system, kings and queens descended from the House of Orange were aided and advised by elected officials from different parts of the Netherlands. For the next 125 years, from 1815 until 1940, Holland was at peace and became one of the most stable and prosperous countries in Europe.

When not threatened by invaders, the Dutch have waged an ongoing battle against the sea. In the first century A.D., the Roman governor Pliny the Elder described people living on dunes which they had piled higher than the ocean tides—"like sailors on a ship, when the tide is high."[1] The word *holland,* the informal name of the country, means "soaked land."

Like many parts of Holland, Amsterdam once was marshland. It began as a fishing village, with a single dam across the Amstel River—thus the name, from the word *Amstelredamme.* Fish traders settled there, and the town expanded after the 1100s. It became an official chartered city in 1300.

To develop Amsterdam and other populated areas, the Dutch had to prevent floods and to reclaim (drain) land that became flooded. A spirit of industriousness and cooperation grew as people built many dams, called dykes, to hold back water. Windmills were commonly used to drain land until engines and other mechanical pumps took over this job in modern times.

The North Sea threatened the land, but it was also an asset for a small country with few natural resources. The sea held herring and other valued seafood, and it allowed Holland to build a successful trading economy. The port of Amsterdam grew steadily as Dutch sailors became expert navigators and shipbuilders. During

A row of houses overlooks one of the canals that crisscross the city of Amsterdam.

the Middle Ages, sailors ventured to Portugal for salt and crossed the Baltic for timber. By the late 1500s, coffee, tea, spices, sugar, pepper, cocoa, rubber, silk, and diamonds could be found there. From Amsterdam, these goods could be shipped further into Europe along Holland's main rivers: the Rhine (from Germany) and the Maas and the Scheldt (both from Belgium). Water travel was also possible within the city. A system of canals and bridges developed to unite the pieces of land that made up the city of Amsterdam, resulting in its nickname, "the Venice of the North."

During the 1600s, Amsterdam played a major role in Holland's Golden Age. Trade and new territory in America and other lands had made Holland a world power, and Amsterdam was its largest city. The arts flourished there, and the University of Amster-

A thriving port city for more than 400 years, Amsterdam's docks bustle with ships loading and unloading cargo.

dam, founded in 1632, attracted distinguished professors in law, theology, and the sciences. A prosperous middle class developed.

Holland developed a feature which was then unique in Europe: religious tolerance. Once oppressed for his Protestant religious beliefs, William of Orange had established religious liberty in Holland when he ruled during the late 1500s. During those years, Jews were being persecuted in Spain, Portugal, and other countries. Many Jews moved to Holland, the only European nation that gave them equal rights. They called Amsterdam a *mokum*—safe city. Religious freedom also attracted Protestants from Catholic-dominated France and Belgium. The English-born Pilgrims lived in Holland for 12 years before founding Plymouth Colony in Massachusetts in 1620. The Jewish-Dutch philosopher Baruch Spinoza wrote of Amsterdam in the mid-1600s: "In this flourishing republic, this city second to none, men of every nation and every sect live together in the utmost harmony...."[2] By then, half of Amsterdam's residents were immigrants.

Immigration continued during the 1700s, giving the city a diverse population that learned to live together peacefully, although people still often lived and socialized with their own ethnic and religious groups. Amsterdam was especially diverse—Holland had the largest Jewish population. Immigrants brought special skills, among them diamond-cutting, which made Amsterdam into the world center of the industrial-diamond-cutting industry.

During the early 1800s, Napoleon Bonaparte visited Amsterdam, which he named the "third city" in his Empire, after Paris and Rome. He was impressed by the city's 290 bridges and by the number of languages, including German and French, that many Dutch could speak. His wife, Marie Louise, admired the tulips and other flowers, for by then Holland grew and exported top-quality bulbs.

In 1939, the bicycle was the favorite means of transportation for many Amsterdammers.

In the late 1800s, Amsterdam was known both for its charm and commerce. Historian Geoffrey Cotterell gives a view of the city from the Ij River:

> In the foreground there was a flotilla of little boats and steamers, busy loading or unloading or hooting for late passengers. There was noise and activity everywhere, cranes creaked, dockers worked, the quay was alive with people, horses, wagons, omnibuses. Behind them were the tall, tapering, narrow, gabled houses, painted in somber colors but with hundreds of white framed windows like eyes watching the port's activity, and beyond the rooftop line there was a vague impression of towers and domes shaped in Oriental or Spanish fashion.[3]

By 1890, the view changed somewhat, after the Central Railway was built, and bicycles made with the newly invented air tire became popular.

Holland did not fight in World War I (1914-1918), declaring itself neutral. Even so, Amsterdam's sea trade dwindled because German mine fields and U-boats made the North Sea hazardous. There were coal and food shortages, as Holland traded food in exchange for scarcer supplies of German coal.

After the war, Amsterdam regained its sea trade and reputation as a quiet and comfortable place to live. Holland did not suffer from the physical or economic damage that plagued France, Germany, and other participants in World War I. The Dutch currency (the guilder) was sound, and agricultural and dairy products were plentiful. Meals featured bread, cheese, meat, chicken, vegetables, marmalade, milk, and butter—enough for both sides of the bread. Children enjoyed chocolate in beverages, candies, and as flakes called "hailstones" which were spread on buttered bread. There was enough food after World War I that middle-class Dutch families housed and fed undernourished children from Germany, Austria, and other war-torn countries until they grew healthy enough to return home.

Amsterdammers usually lived in tall, narrow apartments, often part of block-long brick buildings. Orange roofs sloped above lace-curtained windows at both the front and back of the apartment. Window boxes held plants and seasonal flowers. The buildings faced canals or cobbled streets, lined with elm, poplar, and chestnut trees. Sparrows, pigeons, and seagulls swooped around the city.

Stores sold stylish clothing and other goods, while open markets offered foods and flowers. Theaters showed American, British, and German films. Bicycles were the most common way to travel, both for essential trips and for fun. Whole families rode together, using small carriers for children too young to handle their own bicycle. Electric streetcars, canal ferries, and automobiles provided other forms of transportation.

When not in school, young people enjoyed bicycling, dance clubs, sleepover parties, table tennis, tennis, and summer swims at the Amstelpark pool. They went to movies and ice cream parlors. When the canals froze, people of all ages donned wooden skates for Holland's traditional winter sport. Afterward, they sipped hot chocolate or anise-flavored milk from an outdoor stall.

After Adolf Hitler seized power in Germany in 1933, German Jews were singled out for harsh persecution, so many left the country. As in past centuries, thousands of Jewish refugees settled in Amsterdam, where Jews were part of all social classes and professions. Among these German refugees was the family of Otto Frank, whose daughter Anne later wrote a famous diary about her life in hiding during the Nazi Occupation.

During the 1930s, a Dutch Nazi Party, called the NSB, was formed in Holland. Historian Walter Maass found that it drew a few

A group of young Dutch Nazi Party (NSB) supporters hold a parade through the streets of Amsterdam.

thousand members before the war. As in other places, the Nazis established Boys and Girls clubs. "NSB-ers" were often ridiculed by other Dutch. Amsterdammer Jan Jonkheer, age 14, wrote of the one Nazi boy in his classroom whom other students called "Klaus the Rat." In 1936, 12,000 people in Amsterdam attended an anti-Nazi rally called "Unity through Democracy."

In March 1938, the Dutch radio reported that Hitler had marched triumphantly into Vienna, Austria. Miep Gies, a young woman living in Amsterdam, wrote that she and her friends of different religions discussed their outrage when they heard about the actions of the Nazis: "Viennese Jews were made to clean out public toilets and to scrub the streets in an orgy of Nazi depravity [and their] possessions had been seized...."[4]

A country of readers, interested in politics, the Dutch followed current events by reading and discussing the daily newspapers. They were shocked again in December 1938 after reading about a massive anti-Jewish demonstration in Germany called *Kristallnacht*—Crystal Night, "the night of broken glass." Jewish people had been violently attacked; their synagogues, shops, and homes had been vandalized, burned, and destroyed. Dutch citizens of various classes and religions contributed more than 500,000 guilders (about $250,000 at the time) to aid the victims of Crystal Night. Alarmed, Amsterdam's million citizens, of whom nearly 10% were Jewish, watched the Nazis, with their policies of racial and religious hatred, forcing their way across Europe.

When World War II broke out in 1939, Amsterdam's sea trade was disturbed again. Dutch ships struggled to avoid explosives the Germans had placed in the North Sea, and the British blockade interrupted German-Dutch trade. Gasoline and sugar were rationed, while imported goods cost more and were harder to get.

Throughout 1939, there were rumors that Hitler would invade Holland, despite its neutrality. The small Dutch army prepared for possible attacks. Troops moved horse-drawn artillery across fields that had been flooded, in case Holland opened its dykes to slow down the invaders. Foot soldiers carrying machine guns practiced crossing frozen fields on ice skates. Jan Jonkheer wrote that his father had been called to his reserve unit: "But I am sure this mobilization is a false alarm, because Hitler has promised faithfully not to invade Holland."[5]

Fears rose in April 1940 when Hitler invaded neutral Denmark and Norway, yet May arrived without incident. Amsterdam was in bloom with tulips, hyacinths, and daffodils. On May 9, Jan wrote in his diary about plans for the next day, his fourteenth birthday:

> We will begin my birthday with a tour of the city by boat, gliding through the grachten [canals]. Then we will go to the Rijksmuseum, which is our national gallery. It makes me proud to be Dutch when I look at the paintings by Frans Hals, Jan Steen, Vermeer, and especially Rembrandt....We will have lunch at Zandvoort aan Zee. I like this seaside resort. In the evening we are going to Haarlem, because there is to be an organ recital in Saint Bavo Church....The weatherman says it is going to be fine tomorrow. Hurrah![6]

The next day, Jan and the rest of Amsterdam awoke in a changed country, destined to suffer through five years of Nazi occupation.

★ ★ ★

German troops cross the border into Holland on May 10, 1940.

★★★★★★★★★★

2

INVASION AND SURRENDER

At about 4:15 A.M., on Friday, May 10, 1940, the people of Amsterdam were awakened by strange noises. Miep Gies recalls, "I heard what sounded like a persistent humming noise...then the noise was mixed with a faraway muted sound of thunder....Downstairs, someone was turning the static-filled dial of the radio. My heart began to pound. What was happening?"[1] Elsewhere in Amsterdam, people heard rumbling sounds. Still in their nightclothes, they ran into the streets and climbed onto roofs to investigate.

Jan Jonkheer's mother woke him. He wrote in his diary: "One look at her serious face and I knew that something was wrong. She kissed me and said, 'Happy Birthday,' but it was so unlike my mother, who is a very jolly person....I could now hear the distant thuds. 'What is it?' I asked. [She said] 'The Germans have invaded Holland. I pray for Father, and for our poor country.'"[2] Jan's father was in the Dutch army reserves.

People turned on their radios or went to a neighbor's home to hear that Hitler had invaded Holland and Belgium without even a declaration of war. The Nazi air force, the Luftwaffe, had launched a vigorous attack, dropping parachutists disguised in Dutch army uniforms, along with guns and equipment. Queen Wilhelmina issued a fierce protest, calling the attack a "flagrant breach of conduct."[3] Radio announcers said:

> German forces are attacking Dutch airfields and munitions dumps....Nazi air-borne troops have parachuted onto the airfields of Holland and have overpowered the Dutch air force. German armies have driven across the southern provinces of Limburg and Noord-Brabant into Belgium and are advancing along the Rhine and Maas rivers toward Rotterdam.

The broadcast ended with the Dutch national anthem.

Citizens of Amsterdam read notices of the German invasion.

While the ill-equipped Dutch army struggled against the invaders, people waited for news. Throughout Holland, people expressed shock, anger, sorrow, and fear. Unsure what to do, many people in Amsterdam went to work as usual. There were air-raid sirens during the day as the shelling and bombing continued.

People gathered near radios for information. They were told to stay indoors, to discard alcoholic beverages that German soldiers might drink, and to tape windows so they would not be shattered by bombing. A Dutch woman named Corrie ten Boom later wrote that "advice, rolls of adhesive, and tales of the night's terror passed from door to door."[4] An eight o'clock curfew was set, and people bought blackout paper to cover their windows during the night. Shoppers crowded into butcher shops, bakeries, and greengroceries to buy extra food. Those who ventured out raced into the nearest doorway when they heard a plane. After doing errands, people hurried home, where they felt most safe.

Amsterdam's movie houses and theaters were closed, along with schools, offices, and many stores. No mail was delivered, and only hospitals and military personnel were allowed to use the telephone. The streets and canals were unnaturally quiet as trucks, buses, taxis, streetcars, and ferries stood idle. Newspapers were thinner than usual.

Outside Amsterdam, people also felt fearful, angry, and confused. In Rotterdam, 12-year-old Dirk van der Heide wrote:

About fifty [parachutists] came down at once....Uncle Pieter said, "The damned ungrateful swine. We took their war babies and fed them and this is what we get back." Some of the German planes dropped pieces of paper...[saying] the Germans came as friends and were sorry to be doing what they were doing but they had to protect us from the English and the French. This made everyone laugh at first and made them angry too. The paper also said that we should stop fighting for it was foolish and crazy....Why did we want to fight against our friends the Germans? the paper said. "Our friends the Germans," Mijnheer van Helst said, spitting. He stuck the paper on the wall and ran his pencil through it.[5]

In Rotterdam, as elsewhere, Dutch men searched for Germans and Dutch Nazis. For protection, Dirk said, "A few people have tin or steel helmets like the soldiers but I wore a kettle over my head and so did many other people."[6] In many areas, there was no drinking water or electricity. Citizens helped to rescue others who were trapped in burning or collapsed buildings.

Queen Wilhelmina and Prince Bernhard in England

The Dutch had not fought a war for more than 100 years. With few tanks and only 125 aircraft, Holland's armed forces were no match for thousands of well-trained German soldiers with modern bombers, tanks, and other equipment. Radio reports indicated that despite some help from French and Belgian troops and the British Royal Air Force, Holland was losing one battle after another during the two days after the initial invasion.

Another news bulletin left many people feeling surprised and dejected: The queen, her family, and the cabinet had escaped from The Hague, the Dutch seat of government, to London aboard British warships, after removing the gold from the Dutch treasury. Jan Jonkheer wrote, "For a moment it looked like desertion, but, as my mother explained to me, the struggle against Hitler will be carried

To slow down the advancing German tanks, the Dutch built roadblocks across many of the streets.

on from there...."[7] Other Amsterdammers also realized that if their leaders had remained in Holland, the government itself could have been held captive by the Nazi invaders. Their rulers could help more by running a government in exile. Soon, the radio brought the heartening news that Princess Juliana's husband, Prince Bernhard, was fighting with Dutch troops in Zeeland in southern Holland.

Although the Germans were winning, they were encountering more resistance in Holland than they had expected. On May 12, the German commander in the region of Rotterdam, the capital of South Holland, received a telegram saying that resistance there: MUST BE BROKEN AT ALL COSTS. IF NECESSARY THREATEN DESTRUCTION OF THE CITY AND CARRY IT OUT.

By then, Dutch commanders realized that they had little hope of ousting the invaders. When they heard that the Germans might bomb Rotterdam, a Dutch officer met with a German officer on the afternoon of May 14 to discuss a surrender. Their meeting had just ended when both saw German bombers fly overhead. Radio communication to the planes failed to work, and the 54 German Stukas proceeded to devastate Rotterdam.

Water mains burst, and fires destroyed 750 city blocks. When it was over, 900 people were dead, thousands were injured, and 78,000 were homeless. Dirk van der Heide witnessed the bombing:

> The worst air raid of all has just come....One bomb landed on the lawn by our air shelter and one side of the shelter is caved in....The whole house rocked when the bombs came close. We put our fingers in our ears but it didn't help much....I went out for a while and they were taking dead people out of the bombed houses....There is a funny smell in the air like burnt meat and a funny yellow light all over the country from the incendiary bombs. Three men were killed trying to get a bomb away that hadn't gone off yet. One of the men was our postmaster and I loved him very much. He gave me my first bicycle

ride. It is awful to watch the people standing by their bombed houses. They just walk around and look at them and look sad and tired.[8]

In contrast, a German who flew one of the bombers described "a splendid picture of invincible strength."[9]

Hearing that Rotterdam had been destroyed, people in Amsterdam were aghast. They learned that Germany had threatened to bomb other Dutch cities, starting with Utrecht and Amsterdam. The Dutch commander, General Henri Winkelman, told his officers: "To save the population and avoid further bloodshed, I believe I am justified in ordering the troops under your command to stop fighting."[10] A formal surrender was signed on May 15, just five days after the German invasion. General Winkelman spoke over Dutch radio, urging people to stay as calm as possible.

Most Dutch agreed that more fighting would lead to heavy damage and casualties, with the Germans still winning in the end. There was some panic among the Jews, German refugees, and well-known anti-Nazis. The fire department got extra calls, as people had accidents while burning anti-Nazi books and papers.

Jews living in Amsterdam were horrified at the prospect of Nazi control. Some joined other anti-Nazis who were trying to flee from Holland by boat. But the Amsterdam harbors were blocked, mine fields were in the sea, and gasoline tanks near the North Sea Canal were ablaze. Leesha Rose, a 17-year-old Jewish girl, heard some family friends describe the scene at Ijmuiden Harbor:

> We, together with thousands of people, were rushing on the highway by car and by bicycle. Some highways were blocked by the Germans....The German planes were circling above the sea and shooting at the full boats and we saw people falling into the water. People were clamoring impatiently to escape, offering money and jewelry for a place on a boat. But only a few boats got away.[11]

Like others, the Roses' friends had to return, to an uncertain future. As German refugees, they had seen how the Nazis tormented the Jews. Leesha Rose wrote, "The following day we heard that Mr. and Mrs. Prinz were found dead. They had committed suicide."[12]

Few of the small boats that left Amsterdam managed to reach England. In one story with a happy ending, a Dutch woman succeeded in taking five cars full of Jewish orphans from Amsterdam to the ship *Bodegraven,* which took them safely to England.

Everywhere, people asked worried questions: What would the Nazis do? How would they treat the Dutch? Leesha Rose had planned to start college in the fall. Now she wondered, "What would become of our beautiful, peaceful country? Would we be able

Triumphant German troops enter Amsterdam.

A German jeep rolls into Amsterdam shortly after the invasion.

to continue our comfortable, relaxed, and orderly way of life?"[13] Miep Gies expressed the rage felt by many: "Now, suddenly, our world was no longer ours....Nothing worse could happen to us; we were no longer free."[14]

Amsterdammers took pride in their hard-won independence from foreign rulers and their traditions of freedom and tolerance. Now they found themselves in the grip of a dictatorship known for oppression and bigotry. On May 15, as Holland surrendered, Nazi troops paraded through the cities. Wearing helmets and heavy black boots, German soldiers marched through Amsterdam, over the Berlage Bridge and on to the Dam Square. Some followers of the

Dutch Nazis, led by Anton Mussert, cheered and gave the troops cigarettes, flowers, and chocolates.

Jan Jonkheer and his family were among those who stayed home that day. Others stood watching the procession of troops and military equipment. Leesha Rose recalled the armored cars, guns,

The fierce Green Police

panzerwagons, and trucks, followed by rows of stiffly marching soldiers, "their boots lifting and falling on the pavement in minutest cadenza and precision, their arms swaying up and down like a machine....Fear and rage rose within my throat....What was in store for us now?"[15]

Throughout Holland, Nazi soldiers lowered the red, white, and blue Dutch flag and replaced it with the red and black Nazi swastika flag. Soldiers posted signs and brightly colored posters urging young men to join the German army.

Ida Vos was 8 years old that day in 1940. She later wrote about how she felt while watching the victorious Nazis:

> German soldiers are parading through the Dutch streets....They are marching and singing songs that have words I don't understand. "They're going to kill all the Jews!" shouts my mother. I am afraid. I have a stomachache. I am Jewish.[16]

A Nazi standard replaces the Dutch flag outside a building in Amsterdam.

A Nazi propaganda banner proclaims: "Victory for Germany, winning for Europe on all fronts."

3

THE NIGHTMARE BEGINS

As the Occupation began, distressing news came from abroad: Belgium and Luxembourg had also been defeated, and France was rapidly losing ground. People in Amsterdam tried to resume their daily activities, going to work and to school, while German planes buzzed overhead. Workmen repaired damaged bridges and water pipes. People from Rotterdam came to the capital seeking shelter—in all, 386 Dutch communities helped to house these thousands of homeless people. In rural areas near Amsterdam, farmers drained acres of flooded land and searched for wandering livestock.

Now there were German soldiers and police, called "Green Police," because they wore green uniforms, in the city's cafes, restaurants, and theaters. The people called them *Moffen,* the name of certain packaged biscuits shaped like pigs. German-language signs appeared on trees and in newspapers. A headquarters for the Gestapo—the Nazi police—was set up in south Amsterdam, in a former school.

As they encountered the Nazis, many Amsterdammers showed their hostility, early signs of the stubborn Dutch opposition that would continue throughout the Occupation. Historian Adriaan Barnouw wrote how his fellow citizens used "the cold stare, the stony silence, the pretended stupidity, the clearing of the throat, the coughlike chuckle"[1] to annoy the Germans. Berend Beins, who was working as an engineer in Holland when the war began, recalls that "when a German boarded a streetcar, one by one, every Dutch passenger turned his or her back to him."[2]

*Arthur
Seyss-Inquart*

At the end of May, two weeks after Holland's defeat, red-bordered, printed announcements were posted on notice boards in Amsterdam and throughout the country: I HAVE TODAY TAKEN OVER THE CIVIL AUTHORITY OF THE NETHERLANDS. Austrian Arthur Seyss-Inquart had been installed as Reichskommissar of Holland, at an elaborate ceremony in The Hague. Seyss-Inquart was to carry out Hitler's direct orders from Berlin.

The installment of a civil occupation sharpened fears, for such administrations tended to be much worse for a conquered nation than a military occupation. Unlike some military personnel, who had been drafted, civil officials such as Seyss-Inquart were typically zealous Nazis who admired Hitler and agreed with his racist and anti-Semitic opinions.

Seyss-Inquart told the Dutch that their rights and laws would be honored: "Certain measures will be taken, but only insofar as the circumstances will make them necessary...." He claimed that Germany was fighting "a decisive battle for existence, a struggle forced upon it by the hatred of its enemies. That struggle obliges the German nation to stake all its strength...and entitles it to use every means at its disposal...."[3]

With his flashing eyeglasses and severe limp, Seyss-Inquart did nothing to intensify fears during his first weeks in Holland, nor did the Nazi soldiers. But people in Amsterdam worried as new rules took effect daily, and they heard the soldiers sing *"Wir fahren gegen Engelland"*—"We are sailing to fight against England"—during their drills.

On June 4, Jan Jonkheer wrote that Germans visited his school:

> The Nazis are trying all their tricks to win over the schoolchildren. They have given us sweets which most of us have put in the drain, and they have allowed the top class to matriculate without passing the exams. Our teacher says, "Be brave. Hold your heads up."[4]

That night, the BBC (British Broadcasting Corporation) radio station announced that British troops had lost a strenuous battle in northern Belgium. Thousands of Allied soldiers had been stranded on beaches around Dunkirk, helplessly awaiting the Germans. Naval and civilian small craft managed to rescue 337,000 of the men and evacuate them to England. Speaking of "the miracle at Dunkirk," the new British prime minister, Winston Churchill, told listeners from Allied countries:

> We shall fight...on the beaches and oceans. We shall fight...in the air....We shall fight on the landing grounds. We shall fight in the fields and on the streets. We shall never surrender.

Trapped in occupied Holland, listening to the BBC behind blacked-out windows, many Amsterdammers found Churchill's words inspiring and hoped that, somehow, the Allies could win.

Queen Wilhelmina also encouraged people through broadcasts on the BBC. Shortly after escaping to England, she announced that the Free Dutch Government would operate from there and that the Dutch should resist in any way they could; Holland would be free again someday.

In June, Seyss-Inquart disbanded both houses of Parliament. It was *verboten*—forbidden—to display the Dutch flag, national colors, or pictures of the royal family. Yet on June 29, thousands of people in Amsterdam openly celebrated the birthday of Prince Bernhard by wearing a white carnation (his favorite flower), orange ribbons, and red, white, and blue insignia. Jan Jonkheer said this made the Nazis "furious; to our delight, they have issued an order, 'Tear every carnation from buttonhole or dress.'"[5] Jan and his teenage friends did not back away, because, like many others, they had hidden pieces of razor blades in their flowers. A Dutch youth group, the National Youth League, played a large role in organizing the day's events. After hearing this, the Nazis banned the group.

July brought more restrictions. It was illegal to listen to any radio station except the official German one, which controlled the news and played only German music. Nonetheless, Radio Orange—a Dutch station—began broadcasts from London in late July. People began listening regularly, in secret. Amsterdam's movie theaters now showed only German films, and the newspapers could print nothing negative about Germany. People were forbidden to strike from their jobs or distribute pamphlets that promoted resistance.

Still, people engaged in nonviolent acts of resistance. Amsterdam contained many small presses and skilled printers. They be-

gan to print underground newspapers—secret newssheets that told people about the progress of the war and offered advice about coping with the Nazi regime. Besides articles, there were pictures of the royal family and cartoons that ridiculed the Germans. The papers had to be hidden because Seyss-Inquart had forbidden any material he considered "likely to disturb the public order and safety" or "contrary to the national requirements."[6]

Dutch patriots buy white carnations to wear on the birthday of Prince Bernhard on June 29, 1940.

Resistance fighters print an underground newssheet.

To commemorate the July birthday of Queen Emma, who had died in 1934, Dutch housewives washed their flags and hung them out to dry. Throughout Amsterdam, red, white, and blue flags fluttered on clotheslines, in full view of the Nazis. People assembled near a statue of the late queen until the Green Police dispersed them.

Along with the suppression of democratic government came economic restraints. Prices on various goods were fixed, and people needed special permits to use cars or motorcycles. The Nazis began exporting Dutch gasoline and raw materials to Germany. When taking Dutch goods, the Germans "paid" with paper banknotes called "Reich's credit bills," token money that Hitler's government claimed could later be exchanged for Dutch money. The Nazis also demanded that people trade their gold and personal coins (about $72 million worth by the war's end) for these credit notes.

Amsterdammers learned that the Nazis had emptied the Netherlands Bank and were stripping the city of other valuables. Because Amsterdam was a world diamond-cutting center, the Nazis had found and seized many pounds of industrial diamonds. Several owners of large diamond-cutting firms, among whom were prominent Jews, hastily buried or hid their diamonds. A Nazi commander stole paintings from the gallery of a famous Jewish art expert who had died while trying to escape by sea.

Soon it was clear that the Germans were taking food—tons of coffee, tea, cocoa, butter, milk, vegetable oils, produce, and meats. Historian Louis de Jong found that almost all the 1940 Dutch apple harvest went to Germany, and that "tens of thousands of cattle and horses, and poultry by the millions, made the trip eastwards...never to return."[7] Holland's rail and water connections made such transfers possible for the Nazis.

At first, the Dutch were urged, but not forced, to work for the German war effort. The Nazis expected that by changing Holland's government and public institutions, they could lead the Dutch to share their goals. Hitler had long regarded most Dutch as part of a light-skinned group of people he called Aryans. In his plan, Aryans would multiply to become a "master race." The Nazis foresaw a new Holland, part of a mighty German empire.

Toward that end, the Nazis began propaganda efforts throughout Holland. The signs on the Royal Palace and other public buildings in Amsterdam were changed, with the Nazis substituting the word "National" wherever "Royal" had been. In the summer of 1940, the Nazis removed books they did not like from libraries and bookshops. They changed school textbooks and courses to fit their ideology. Elizabeth Isakson recalls feeling "frustrated and angry"[8] when the Nazis banned English and French language courses at her school. Many books, including several written in English, were burned, and Nazi newspapers were widely distributed. Dutch Nazis were ordered to sell these papers and to march often to show their strength.

A Dutch street sign is replaced by a German one.

Much propaganda was aimed at young people. Hitler had said that he hoped to develop youth "from whom the world will shrink back. A violently active, dominating, intrepid, brutal youth—this is what I am after. Youth must be...indifferent to pain. There must be no weakness or tenderness in it."[9]

In August, tensions rose when Amsterdam's German-Jewish refugees were told to register at the local aliens' office. Although fearful, the Jews complied and nothing else happened to them at that time. Nazi propaganda steadily came to the city in the form of radio programs, movies, newspapers, and books. Much of it was clearly meant to arouse hostility toward Jews and to divide the Dutch people along religious and political lines.

Amsterdam was a religiously integrated city, so the Nazis faced strong opposition. Marion Pritchard, a Dutch college student during the war, wrote of a Nazi newsreel that was shown throughout Holland:

> I remember a film called *The Eternal Jew*. I attended it with a group of friends, some fellow students at the school of social work, some Jewish, some Gentile. It was so crude, so scurrilous, that we could not believe anybody would take it seriously, or find it convincing.[10]

During August, hundreds of German bombers droned above Amsterdam as they headed across the English Channel. The BBC reported that London was being bombed repeatedly. As the end of the month approached, the Nazis strictly forbade any display of flags, carnations, national symbols, or the color orange on Queen Wilhelmina's birthday, August 31. They had also ordered people not to grow or wear any orange-colored flowers, marigolds, white carnations, or forget-me-nots, saying that such flowers "would be considered attempts at provoking forbidden demonstrations."[11]

Nonetheless, on August 31, the Amsterdam Municipal Theater flew the American and House of Orange flags side by side. British planes dropped orange-colored pamphlets and confetti, to the delight of the people. That night, British planes staged an orange fireworks display above Amsterdam, while the Green Police ordered onlookers to go home at once.

The joy of that day was short-lived. In the fall of 1940, the Nazis dismissed Jewish Civil Service workers and other public officials, including postal workers, teachers, and professors. In October, businesses owned or partly owned by Jews were forced to register with the government; then Jews were ordered to sell the businesses at unfairly low prices. Jews were forbidden to buy property. Non-Jews—Gentiles—were ordered to sign official papers, called "Aryan Declarations," saying they were not Jewish.

The Nazis rationalized their actions: "The orders against the Jews are not an interference in internal Dutch relations. They are only directed against the Jews, who are considered enemies of Germany."[12]

Leesha Rose wrote:

> The decrees and orders against us were meant to destroy our pride and self-esteem....To refuse to carry out the Nazi decrees would be at the risk of being punished, imprisoned, or killed. Some Jews tried to evade the decrees but few succeeded. It was the individual Jew against the mighty Nazi military power. With keen psychological precision, they gradually stripped us of our rights, our social standing, and our worldly possessions....[13]

Some Jews decided to go immediately into hiding, joining other *onderduikers,* or "divers." But Holland is a flat, open country with no mountains and only 7% of its land forested, so natural hiding places were scarce. In 1940, about 9 million Dutch were crowded into 33,000 square miles of land, surrounded by open sea or by carefully guarded borders. Jews and other people hunted by the Nazis had to get false identity papers—a difficult task—or rely on brave people to hide them in homes, barns or other buildings.

As oppression increased, Amsterdam's church leaders spoke more openly against the Nazi administration. Throughout Holland, religious groups protested, even though they knew that in Germany, anti-Nazi church leaders had been imprisoned and even killed. The Nazis had harassed Catholic nuns and priests, closed religious

Green Police check the identity papers of Dutch citizens.

schools, and censored church literature. As an added insult, Hitler Youth marches were held on Sundays.

The General Assembly of Reformed Churches (Protestant) submitted resolutions to Seyss-Inquart. They pledged allegiance to the House of Orange and said they would continue to pray for the queen. In another letter, they protested the dismissal of Jewish civil servants, saying, "We are profoundly moved by the meaning of these measures, touching as they do, upon important spiritual interests and being against Christian mercy...."[14]

A ration book

On Sunday, November 10, Amsterdam's Catholic priests read a clerical letter telling their parishioners that "the world is threatened by a nationalistic and materialistic outlook in which there is no place for Christ."[15] The church said that Nazis would not be allowed to receive Catholic sacraments, marry at the altar, or be buried on church grounds. No Nazi badges, flags, or uniforms would be permitted at Catholic funeral processions.

As Jews were being singled out for persecution, the general living conditions also declined. The Nazis began rationing certain foods and other goods during the fall of 1940. By showing an identity card, people got weekly ration coupon books from government offices. Coupons showed the specific amounts of particular foods that one could buy. All cloth goods were rationed, so, from then on, people made hard choices. Buying new socks or underwear

42

meant giving up a raincoat, pajamas, or other clothing and blankets or household items. Special permits were needed to buy shoes and winter coats.

The 1940-1941 winter was again harsh, but this year Amsterdam had far less heat. Dutch coal was being shipped to German homes, factories, and railroads. Schools and public buildings in Amsterdam sometimes closed for lack of fuel. People tried substituting gas and electricity until the Nazis restricted those too. The Amsterdam Health Department demanded extra fuel for households with sick people or infants. Whole wooded areas disappeared as people chopped down trees to burn for warmth.

In addition, the Nazis raised taxes and lowered many people's wages. They imposed a 4.5% "victory tax" on all wages and increased taxes on businesses, forcing some business owners to pay nearly 90% of their income in taxes. Price-fixing forced some shop owners to sell products below what they had cost. Understandably, many businesses closed.

As the cold days dragged on, the Nazis announced that all Jews in Amsterdam must register with the census office. Tensions rose in February when Nazis attacked Jews living in South Amsterdam. After several fights occurred, the Nazis sealed off the area by raising the bridges and posting signs. Soldiers were stationed around the quarter. Angered by the violent attacks and other anti-Jewish laws, Christian neighbors used pipes and whatever other weapons they could find to help Jews fight off the Nazis.

The Germans retaliated by viciously arresting 425 young Jewish men in Amsterdam in a *razzia,* a Dutch word for roundup, and shipping them by truck to a prison camp called Mauthausen. The men's families soon heard that they had died accidentally or from illnesses or heart attacks—stories the Dutch did not believe.

One of the many razzias the Green Police held on Jewish citizens.

Angry about the deaths at Mauthausen, Amsterdam's dock-workers led a citizens' group calling for a general strike. Dutch workers on bicycles delivered pamphlets, saying, "We are striking on behalf of the Jews, will you join?"[16] The strike began on February 25 and lasted three days. Inspired by the dockworkers, people from all social and economic classes defied the Nazis and stopped working. In Amsterdam, transportation and city services came to a sudden stop. Shops, factories, offices, and schools were deserted.

The February strike was unique: It was the only time that so many people in an occupied European country demonstrated forcefully against the persecution of Jews. German soldiers were told to end the strike by using all necessary force. They began firing at people on the streets, and they arrested more than 3,000 people. A number of Amsterdam's dockworkers and others were sent to concentration camps.

The strike had shown that unarmed civilians could not withstand the brute force of the Nazi soldiers. Yet the morale of the people improved briefly as they overcame fear to express their rage and contempt. Leesha Rose wrote that she and many other Jewish citizens "felt grateful to the strikers and proud that they had responded so strongly and had fought on our behalf."[17]

As spring 1941 approached, it was clear that the Nazis intended to persecute Jews and to treat the Dutch people severely. Amsterdam had shown itself to be not only uncooperative but strongly opposed to the Nazi system. The city and its people would pay a heavy price during the next four years of the Occupation.

People in line for food at a public kitchen.

4

INCREASING HARDSHIPS

As spring 1941 arrived, daily life in Amsterdam became increasingly grim. Once standard fare, poultry, meats, butter, bread, cheeses, and produce were no longer plentiful at mealtimes. Steamy cups of hot chocolate, coffee, and tea, as well as sweets, such as cookies and cakes, were rare or not available. There was less to eat and food cost more, often more than ten times what it had cost before 1940. Even when people had ration coupons, they could not always find those foods in the neighborhood stores.

Dutch milk was being shipped to Germany, so the people were limited to one watered-down cup a day for adults and two cups for children, amounts which were steadily reduced as time went on. Cream was skimmed off and could be gotten only with a doctor's prescription. By spring 1941, 15% of Holland's dairies had closed. People were allowed one egg per week. They ate less than one-third as much meat as before and were lucky to get 10 ounces a week. Meanwhile, about 75% of Holland's slaughtered cattle went to Hitler's empire. The Amsterdam city council protested that meat cutbacks would "greatly increase the number of malnutrition cases in our city."[1]

Unlike rural people who grew and raised food, Amsterdammers had to wait for food to be shipped into the city. Often, there were no eggs or dairy products. When there were eggs, they cost about 25 cents each. Elizabeth Isakson says that her mother, who was hospitalized for surgery, "urged me to visit at lunchtime so I could share her egg and cup of whole milk."[2] As rationed amounts of bread, meat, eggs, milk, butter, and oil were cut, many citizens turned to the black market, which sold food and other goods outside the Nazi system. Most Dutch people sold or bought goods in this way at some time during the war.

Conditions deteriorated for everyone, but Jews faced much graver problems. In June 1941, the Nazis ordered Jews to have a large black "J" stamped on their identity cards, which everybody was required to carry at all times. Jews could not use or sell their own property. Seeing the pain of her Jewish friends, Miep Gies writes that "a slow strangulation was taking place, we began to realize: first isolation, and now impoverization."[3]

Then a series of new laws stigmatized Jewish children and cut them off from their usual activities. In August 1941 they were banned from Amsterdam's public schools and ordered to attend newly formed Jewish schools. Ida Vos described how her life changed:

> Suddenly, I am no longer allowed to attend my own school. I am not allowed to go swimming or to play tennis. I am not allowed to go to the library or the movies or to sit outside on a bench. I am not allowed to take a train or to go to a park. The black-and-white signs are everywhere: FORBIDDEN FOR JEWS.[4]

Church organizations kept denouncing the Nazis' actions. Protestant-Reformed officials even advised their members to disobey Nazi decrees contrary to the laws of God:

The entrance to the Jewish Quarter of Amsterdam.

> According to God's Providence, the Jews have lived among us for centuries and are bound up with us in a common history and com-

mon responsibility. Our Saviour's commandment to love our neighbors as we love ourselves, applies to them as it applies to any other neighbor.[5]

When the Nazis did not respond to written requests, Catholic and Protestant clergymen met with Seyss-Inquart. Amsterdammers learned that at one such meeting, church leaders had asked the Nazi commissioner to "recognize the spiritual distress of the Netherlands people and to avoid doing further harm."[6] The clergymen asked that the Nazis stop persecuting Jews and refrain from arresting people for no known crime. They told Seyss-Inquart that they rejected Nazism and all efforts to force it on them, saying, "The resistance of the churches is based on the fact that Nazism assails justice, charity, and freedom of conscience—all of which are inseparable from the Christian faith."[7]

For many Dutch, attempts to "Nazify" them and their children was one of the most repulsive aspects of the war. Johtje Vos, a woman who hid Jewish children from the Nazis, later said:

> In Holland before the war...children were brought up with tolerance and respect for others. Certainly, in my family and my husband's family, we learned that saying something unkind about somebody who had a different race, color, creed, nationality, or whatever, was very wrong and disrespectful.[8]

The Nazis were also having trouble convincing able-bodied Dutch men to work for Germany. With so many German men in the army, the Nazis' need for farm and factory laborers kept rising. German women were told to be homemakers and mothers only, so the Nazis forced their captives—Jews, Poles, gypsies, political prisoners, and men from occupied countries—into labor. By 1941, there were more than a thousand camps in Poland and Germany where people worked for the Nazis until they died or were killed.

Yet only about 120,000 Dutch men, fewer than 6% of those over age 18, were working in German-run factories by 1941—most only after the Nazis threatened to deny their families ration cards.

Certain men, such as farmers and railroad workers, were not told to work in German factories. Food production was so vital that the Nazis removed many young people from school to do farm labor. When a Nazi officer came to Jan Jonkheer's Amsterdam classroom seeking farmhands, Jan and his friend Piet readily volunteered, knowing that the man with the Nazi, Farmer Smit, worked for the Dutch resistance. Jan and Piet received special passes to be outdoors after the 8:00 P.M. curfew, in order to deliver milk and feed farm animals. While delivering food, they transmitted messages and supplies to other resistance workers.

In his diary, Jan wrote about a night that combined resistance work with a trip to deliver beets to a storehouse. After the truckload of beets was unloaded, says Jan, Farmer Smit gave two men:

> four parcels our schoolmaster had given him. Behind the storehouse ran a lonely stretch of railway line. Piet was posted by it half a mile away, and I was posted half a mile the other way. We were to give a low bird call if we saw anything or anybody suspicious. Within five minutes the four parcels were tied to specially chosen points on the railway lines. At ten-thirty, when we were 6 miles away on our return journey, we heard a terrific explosion.[9]

A shortage of farm labor was just one problem that farmers faced. They lacked fertilizer, animal feed, and other supplies, so crop yields were much lower. Their best livestock and work horses were regularly confiscated by the Germans, and the undernourished animals they did raise provided far less milk, eggs, and meat.

These problems all led to further declines in the food supply. By the autumn of 1941, stores in Amsterdam had little meat or dairy products and no coffee, tea, flavorings, or spices. People devised *ersatz*—fake—products. These inferior substitutes included tea made with potato peels and bramble leaves and coffee brewed from barley. Black market coffee cost a whopping $28 a pound.

Imported grains were scarce, so the bakeries no longer sold the tasty rye or wheat breads of the past. Now, potato and other flours were mixed with extra water, resulting in sticky black loaves. About 80% of Holland's produce went to Germany. Amsterdammers flocked to the countryside to buy lettuce, tomatoes, cucumbers, onions, and fruits that had not yet been sold to wholesalers.

Besides quality food and coal, other household items, including soap, were scarce. The soap that was available hurt peoples' skin or was made mostly of clay and did not get things clean. Living without adequate food, fuel, or cleanliness in a densely populated city led to much higher rates of illness and death. In 1941, the death rate for children was 30% to 40% over that in 1939. Contagious diseases, including tuberculosis, polio, diphtheria, influenza, and dysentery, increased during the Occupation.

On December 7, a dramatic news flash came from abroad: The United States had entered the war, after the Japanese launched a surprise bombing attack on the American naval base at Pearl Harbor, Hawaii. The Dutch expressed hope that with America's extensive manpower, munitions, and airplane factories, the Allies could defeat the Nazis. The BBC and Radio Orange also reported encouraging news from Russia, where Hitler's troops had been obstructed by a frigid, muddy winter. Yet the German broadcasts contradicted the BBC and declared that Leningrad and Moscow were about to collapse.

During these battles with Russia, the Nazis ordered people

Members of the resistance examine a shipment of grenades and firearms.

in Amsterdam and elsewhere to turn in their coats, hats, blankets, and gloves for German soldiers at the eastern front. They also raided warehouses and factories for these items. Elizabeth Isakson says that neighbors used specially coded warnings when the Nazis were searching homes: "They would call and say, 'You better put away your fur coat; the moths are getting mine.'"[10]

During the winter of 1941-1942, people had less protection against the cold, as well as a persistent lack of food. Commenting on the 1942 food shortages in Holland, Field Marshal Hermann Goering told his fellow Nazis:

It is not our task to feed a nation which internally alienates itself from us. If this nation is so weak as not to be able to lift its hand—where we don't require its labor—so much the better.[11]

As the winter continued, conflicting reports from the radio and press puzzled the Dutch people, cut off as they were from the world. Some reports said that Jews in occupied Europe were being deported to work camps as slave laborers. Other reports said that Hitler was planning to kill all Jews. Historians note that Jews and Gentiles alike could hardly believe that even the Nazis would really commit some of the rumored atrocities. Reports about the progress of the war also varied, depending on whether they came from an Allied or Nazi source.

More Amsterdammers turned to the underground press, which had been expanding since 1940. Young people on bicycles distributed secret newssheets, including *Vrij Nederland* ("Free Netherlands"), *Het Parool* ("The Password"), and *Trouw* ("Loyalty"). The papers continued to encourage readers and warn them about upcoming restrictions, as well as giving practical advice about hiding things from the Nazis and meeting everyday needs. Underground papers were often placed in sealed envelopes and carried at night, after blackout hours. Henk Aben was among the Dutch young people who delivered them. As he pointed out, "young boys looked innocent."[12] Because the Nazis began confiscating Dutch bicycles from 1942 on, Henk Aben and others tried to make their cycles look clumsy and worn-out in order to keep this vital form of transportation.

Since 1940, young people had proven their value to the Dutch resistance. Using skates or bicycles, they delivered food, radios, messages, money, and other supplies to striking workers, resistance workers, and people living underground. They hid such items inside shoes, school satchels, or the prams they used to walk their younger brothers and sisters along the cobbled streets. Youths engaged in sabotage by blowing up railroad tracks, cutting telephone lines, or painting misleading road signs so that Nazis unfamiliar with parts of Amsterdam would drive into the canals.

Along with Piet and three other friends, Jan Jonkheer formed a group called the SS5. While Jan and Piet worked with Farmer Smit, Charlotte, a 14-year-old fellow SS5 member, got a job as a clerk at Nazi headquarters where she gathered information for the resistance. Because she worked at the Nazi office, Charlotte was shunned by classmates but withstood the criticism to carry out her secret work.

At universities, students went on strike to protest the dismissal of Jewish or anti-Nazi professors and the persecution of fellow students. Some student groups disbanded and formed secret groups when they were told to exclude Jewish members. Students found or helped to build hiding places for people, helped them to move, and supplied food, medical care, and other needs. They registered Jewish babies as Gentiles and got forged ration coupons and other documents.

In May 1942, the Nazis announced yet another rule: All Jews over age five must wear a Jewish star (sometimes called the Star of David; more accurately, the shield of David) made of yellow-colored cloth, with the word JOOD, the Dutch word for Jew, printed in black across the center. The star had to be sewn onto the chest of their clothing and remain visible at all times. Furthermore, Jews were forced to buy the stars with clothing coupons from their ration books.

Irene Butter-Hasenberg, who was 11 years old when this edict took effect, wrote that in Amsterdam:

A Jewish woman wearing the yellow star

> large numbers of gentile people wore the star in the beginning. They felt that if everybody wore the star, it would defeat the purpose. Then, of course, measures were taken against that. So, because the Dutch people reacted that way, they said that wearing the star is a sign of pride; there was a positive association.[13]

Some non-Jews greeted those wearing the star with special courtesy, and people gave up seats to them on public transportation. Henk Aben recalls that his father told him to tip his hat when he encountered someone wearing the star, "to pay your respects."[14]

The Nazis soon began to abuse anyone wearing the cloth star. Irene Butter-Hasenberg remembers how they accosted people on the street who had taken off their coats or jackets (where the stars were sewn) in hot weather, and harassed people for not sewing their stars on precisely enough. She says, "There were more and more incidents of brutality and of beating, shooting, arresting. So every day was fearful. You never knew what would happen."[15]

Most dreadful of all were the mass arrests and deportations of Jews that began in the summer of 1942. Jews over age 15½ received postcards telling them to report at once for deportation to "work camps." The Green Police staged raids in which they drove vans into Amsterdam neighborhoods and arrested people. Jewish victims were told to pack a small suitcase or knapsack with a few belongings, then were forced into the van and taken to the Central Railroad station for the agonizing trip to a Nazi prison camp.

By then, many Jews had been taken from areas surrounding Amsterdam and moved into one section, now a Jewish ghetto, inside the city. Forced to abandon their homes and possessions, hundreds of Jewish families lived in overcrowded buildings, with several families often sharing one stuffy room. Jews had to decide whether to wait and hope they would be overlooked by the Nazis or to go into hiding.

During the Occupation, the total of those in hiding grew to about 300,000. Some people fled to rural areas near Amsterdam, begging farmers to let them stay in barns, other farm buildings, or holes dug under farmyard sheds. Others stayed in Amsterdam. A few people risked hiding in vacant places, but most sought help from friends or resistance workers or asked a trusted acquaintance to help them find a "safe house."

When the Nazis began mass deportations in 1942, the Dutch resistance wrote:

Fellow countrymen: The deportation of all Jewish citizens...is the final link in the long chain of inhuman measures...It means the complete annihilation of the Jews....We must prove our honor is not lost and our conscience is not silenced....We ask our fellow Nederlanders to sabotage all preparations and executions of mass deportations....We expect everyone in the position to do so to sabotage....[16]

Sabotage was difficult, because the Nazis were at their peak of power in 1942 and retaliated brutally when provoked. Jews and Gentiles were even forbidden to associate. People who helped Jews or other hunted people risked being imprisoned, even killed. Yet thousands of people faced the dangers. Important Dutch resistance groups included the National Organization to Help Those in Hiding: *Het Comite* (the committee) founded in 1942 by Utrecht students who specialized in hiding Jewish children; and the Center for Identity Documents, which gave many Jews false identity papers.

People who hid others often relied on grocers, bakers, farmers, and others who knew or guessed what they were doing and managed to give them things that *onderduikers* needed. Why did people risk their lives and share their dwindling food and fuel supplies with strangers? Marion Pritchard said that a shocking event triggered her resistance work:

> One morning on my way to school, I passed a small Jewish Children's home. The Germans were loading the children who ranged in age from babies to 8-year-olds, on trucks. They were upset, and crying. When they did not move fast enough the Nazis picked them up, by an arm, a leg, the hair, and threw them into the trucks. To watch grown men treat small children that way—I couldn't believe my eyes. I found myself literally crying with rage. Two women coming down the street tried to interfere physically, the Germans heaved them into the truck, too....That was the moment I decided that if there was anything I could do to thwart such atrocities, I would do it.[17]

Among those Pritchard helped were a father and his three

A group of Dutch Jews await deportation.

children. Hidden in a friend's home about 20 miles from Amsterdam, the family survived the war.

Johtje Vos, who hid many Jewish children in her house during the Occupation, says that people often ask her if she was afraid. In *The Courage to Care,* she remembers:

> Oh, God, yes! I was scared to death. And very near death also. At one point I was in the hands of the Gestapo, my husband was in jail, and the Nazis were doing a lot of house searching. We were hiding 36 people—32 Jews and four others who also were being sought by the Gestapo. We had made a tunnel underground from our house to a nature reservation, and when we got a warning or had an inkling that the village was surrounded, they all went in there. They all came

through because we had a house in which we could do such things. It was not always easy and often we felt frightened, but we were able to help a little bit, and we did it because we believed it was the right thing to do.[18]

Johannis Boogaard found Jews in need of hiding places and let them stay at his farm. Two Amsterdam women helped him get Jewish children out of the city's orphanage and into hiding. One day, Maurits Cohen was walking down the street with other children from the orphanage when the women approached, and, as Cohen says, "took me out of the line of children into a urinal and they cut off the star...."[19] Cohen was then taken to the Boogaard farm, the first of several places where he hid before the war ended.

Eighteen-year-old Rebecca van Delft served as a courier—one who accompanied Jewish children with false papers—on trains going from Amsterdam to Heerlen, located in southern Holland. She says that as a young woman, she was never asked to show her identification card to a German soldier during these tense trips. Despite the danger, van Delft claims that helping the children was "just a natural thing to do."[20]

Thirteen-year-old Anne Frank wrote a diary about life in hiding with her family and four other people. Anne's father, Otto Frank, had feared that his family might have to hide if the Nazis occupied Holland for very long. He and his wife, Edith, made plans and stored supplies and dried foods, such as beans. The Franks went to their hiding place ahead of schedule, in July 1942, because 16-year-old Margot, Anne's sister, got a "call-up" card from the Nazis. Anne wrote, "Into hiding—where would we go, in a town or the country, in a house or cottage, when, where, how....Margot and I began to pack some of our most vital belongings into a school satchel."[21]

Leaving her beloved pet cat behind, Anne went with her family to what she called the "secret annex," hidden rooms above the Amsterdam warehouse attached to her father's food products business. "We have to whisper and tread lightly during the day, otherwise the people in the warehouse might hear us," Anne wrote. "I can't tell you how oppressive it is never to be able to go outdoors, also I'm very afraid that we shall be discovered and be shot."[22]

The Anne Frank house

Crowded and nervous, the eight people had to rely on friends to provide things they needed and to keep their secret. The young people could not enjoy normal physical activities, school, or friends. Illness was terrifying, because no doctor could come and a cough or sneeze might be heard by someone nearby. *Onderduikers* lived in continual fear of air raids, fire, hunger, or being discovered, as well as fear that the people helping them would be arrested, get sick, or die.

People hiding in regular homes had other places to go hide when Nazi police were conducting their periodic house-by-house searches. These places included closets and secret openings in attics or cellars covered over with fake doors, ceilings, or walls. Herta Montrose-Heymans was 15 years old when she began hiding in various homes in 1942. She said, "We had regular exercises in hiding in certain hiding places which had to be done very, very quickly from the time the bell would go. You were given, say, a minute to hide either in the cupboard or...under the floorboards...."[23]

Life in hiding presented many problems, but more people chose to "dive under" as the Nazi raids increased, day and night. A 1942 underground newspaper described a typical *razzia*:

In the quiet streets of the Zuid [in southern Amsterdam] you hear suddenly the noise of many cars, the hated Green Police vans in which the Germans fetch their victims....They descend from the

Dutch Jews in hiding to escape Nazi persecution.

vans....And then it begins: on each corner stand German agents, rifles slung across their shoulders....And there they noisily climb upstairs: "Are there any Jews living here?" And then the Jews of Holland are driven together on the street corner. Men and women and children....Everybody walking through the neighborhood is stopped at each corner and has to show his identity card. If he has the fatal J on his card he is lost. If not, he can walk on, until another policeman has to be satisfied....The big green vans start their engines and begin to move. The engines keep roaring until a quarter to twelve....The vans bring their loads to the Gestapo Building,...then the transports start leaving the city. It breaks your heart to see people like yourselves hauled away, calm, hopeful, and often dignified....[24]

As deportations of Jews increased, the Dutch church groups again tried unsuccessfully to stop the persecution. One Nazi official told clergymen that the Jews could not stay in Holland but must "return to the place they came from, just as poor as when they left it, covered with lice. Those sympathizing with them will be treated the same way."[25]

The churches could not stop Nazi abuses, but they gave guidance and moral support to many people, so that they had the strength to resist and to help others. Church membership and attendance rose during the war, and extra worship services were held. For many, the church offered a refuge and some stability—both badly needed during the cruelty and uncertainty of those times. As the Occupation entered its final and bleakest years, Amsterdammers used whatever resources they could find within themselves and their community to survive.

★ ★ ★

Boys search garbage cans for scraps of food.

★ ★ ★ ★ ★ ★ ★ ★ ★ ★

5

THE TERRIBLE LAST YEARS

During the last two years of the war, conditions were so grim that surviving from day to day was an ordeal for many people in Amsterdam. Basic needs—food, fuel, clothing, medicine, and health care—were at or below subsistence level. Far worse, for many people, was the emotional strain. There was always the fear, Henk Aben remembers, of the knock on the door, the knock of a dreaded Green Policeman or other Nazi. Elizabeth Isakson recalls, "When I left for school each day, I was never sure whether my home or the other family members would still be there when I returned."[1]   For Jews still living in the ghettoized neighborhoods, there was the constant fear of being deported or arriving home from an errand to find family or friends gone. For those in hiding, there was the fear of being discovered. Those who were helping them worried about being arrested and imprisoned, killed, or sent to a concentration camp.

For men and their families, a new fear had been added: fear of being sent to forced labor. After 1942, the Nazis made a law that every able-bodied man between age 18 and 40 must work for Germany as a soldier or in a military industry. The Germans had tried persuasion for two years, knowing that low wages and unemployment prevented many Dutch men from making a living. Yet most Dutch men stayed home, caring for their families as best they could. A typical ad from a Nazi newspaper said:

> Netherlands' workmen, there is no need for you to be unemployed. You will find plenty to do in Germany. Good pay is awaiting you and you will have the same rights as your German colleagues. Just think—you will be enabled to keep your family well.[2]

Some Dutch men believed such ads and volunteered to go, but they became upset by the living conditions and meager wages. About 25,000 Dutch workers left Germany without permission. They were ordered to return at once or be sentenced to heavy slave labor. The Nazis complained about the Dutch workers' lack of commitment to the war effort. One Nazi official who spoke to Dutch workers at a camp near Munich, Germany, said they were "indifferent...their hands cupped around their heads. Some of them turned their backs upon me...."[3]

When persuasion failed, the Nazis passed the forced labor laws. After September 1943, Nazi police conducted raids in which they abducted men at work, home, church, or from the streets. More than 300,000 Dutch men were forced into labor during the war, in addition to the Dutch Jews sent to labor camps.

Pieter Timmerman was one of many young men who hoped to escape before his eighteenth birthday. He collected wood and metal scraps to make a kayak that would carry him across the North Sea to England, but could not find waterproof material for a cover.

At his draft appointment, he evaded service by pretending to be mentally unfit. Afterward, he worked for the resistance while hiding at a farm.[4]

In *The Other Victims,* Ina Friedman writes about Dirk, who was forced into labor. Dirk was sixteen and had just graduated from trade school as a tool-and-die maker. After the war began, said Dirk,

> Every morning my two brothers, Peter and Bert, and I pedaled our bikes to the tractor repair shop. When we finished, we helped in the garden....We spent our free time playing soccer or in the boys clubs that were run by the church.[5]

One day, Dirk's brothers, riding ahead of him, were pulled off their bicycles by Germans and taken away. In July 1942, Nazis came into the repair shop and seized Dirk along with nine other boys. Dirk recalled, "A neighbor ran to get my mother. She thrust bread and cheese into my hands...."[6] Dirk was taken to Ebenswald labor camp in Berlin. During those harrowing years, he made metal pipes and survived by killing mice and birds for food to supplement the maggot-infested soup served once a day at the camp. He saw many workers die from sickness, malnutrition, and exhaustion. Some were beaten to death or shot.

During the last two years of the war, more Dutch men, fearing forced labor, also went into hiding. People often moved about to avoid being caught. While in hiding, they relied heavily on their inner resources, asking outside friends to bring books, magazines, and newspapers. Reading was one way to escape mentally from the confinement of hiding. Occasionally, *onderduikers* could listen to the BBC or Radio Orange.

Children read, played cards and board games, pursued quiet hobbies, or did needlework to pass the time. At the Boogaard farm, Sara Spier spent hours crocheting: "I made little things to put on the table and I gave them away. I made them from very thin thread because there was not much during the war."[7]

Children tried to keep up with schoolwork. Anne and Margot Frank studied their usual lessons and learned shorthand with a correspondence course brought by an outside friend who had ordered the course in her name. Sara Spier took her schoolbooks with her in hiding: "Every day I did again the last mathematics problems I had at school...but I missed my school very much because I loved to go to school."[8] The safe house in which Bertje Bloch-van Rhijn lived was that of a university friend of her mother's. There were many books for Bertje and her sister to read.

Some children worked on school lessons with their parents, but this was usually not possible. To reduce the risks of being caught, most children were hidden apart from parents and other family members. Adults hiding Jewish children often claimed these young people were cousins or other relatives. Separation from other family members for months and years was a terrible loss, especially for small children.

People kept up their spirits in various ways. For one holiday, Anne Frank could not buy gifts for her family or friends in hiding, so she wrote humorous poems for them. Often, Jews observed their religious holidays. As the months became years, the problems increased. Anne Frank outgrew her clothing and shoes. By 1944, the food supply was also almost gone and those who were helping the Franks could not find enough food in Amsterdam's stores. Anne writes that one night's supper was:

> a hash made from kale which has been preserved in a barrel. It's incredible how much kale can stink when it's a year old!...Ugh! The mere thought of eating that muck makes me feel sick. Added to this, our potatoes are suffering from such peculiar diseases that out of two

buckets...one whole one ends up on the stove....Oh, no, it's no joke to be in hiding during the fourth year of the war. If only the whole rotten business was over![9]

Outside the secret annex and other hiding places, the mass deportations increased after 1943. During some weeks, 3,000 or more Jewish men, women, and children were taken away during raids by the Green Police. Nazis arrived with screeching sirens, to arrest people on the streets or to bang on their doors and force them outside.

A few days after people were arrested, a moving truck from the Puls trucking company came to take away their possessions. With frustration and rage, Amsterdammers watched fellow citizens being abused and forced onto trucks and railcars, their lifetime pos-

Germans load Jews into trucks for deportation to the death camps.

sessions stolen. But they had seen the consequences of interfering with the Nazis. Those who were helping people in hiding had to be especially careful not to show hostility too openly, risking arrest.

People who had family members in hiding or whose homes were sheltering hunted people had been keeping vital secrets under trying circumstances, for years, in some cases. Despite the care taken by those in hiding and their protectors, about 20,000 hidden Jews were found and deported before the war ended. The same number of non-Jews in the resistance were arrested. Some were found by accident; others were the victims of Dutch Nazi informants.

This is what happened to the Frank family and their friends in August 1944. An informant heard suspicious noises and told Nazi police, who raided the secret annex. Otto and Edith Frank were sent to the notorious Auschwitz concentration camp in Poland. There, Edith Frank died of illness in January 1945, and Otto Frank was forced into labor. Anne and Margot went to a filthy, disease-ridden German camp called Bergen-Belsen. Two non-Jewish men who had been helping the Franks were also deported but survived. Miep Gies was taken to Gestapo headquarters that day for questioning and later released. She went back to try to bribe Nazi officials to free the Franks, to no avail. She and her co-worker, Elli, managed to save Anne's diary before Nazis took the Franks' possessions.

As the Germans began to lose the war, they treated people more harshly. Like adult resistance workers, teenagers were sometimes caught and tortured. Pieter Timmerman was arrested, then beaten and interrogated, but another resistance worker bribed the Nazis to release him. Jan and Piet were also caught. Piet was left with a permanent limp, while Jan lost his front teeth and the use of his left arm. They were under age sixteen so the Nazis sentenced them to prison instead of death.

During the gasoline shortage, horses were used to pull trucks.

By 1944, the streets of Amsterdam had about 1% as much traffic as before 1940. Gasoline was scarce, so few taxis or buses ran. People traveled on whatever they could find—stagecoaches, old wagons, horses. Some young people made "cycle taxis"—light wooden structures built over one or more cycles, which they operated with their feet. Cycle taxis could carry passengers about 10 miles per hour.

Few people had bicycles anymore. Dutch people had traveled many miles a day by bicycle, and more than 3 million were used continually before 1940. After the Germans started ordering people to turn in their bicycles in 1942 for military use, they searched homes and buildings for those that were being hidden. Before the war, bicycles had been relatively cheap—about 20 guilders. Now they were 100 guilders (about $50) if they could be found at all. Black market tires cost about twenty times more than usual. By 1944, tires and inner tubes were so scarce that people who had managed to keep their cycles could not replace worn tires or inner

Going in search of food and shelter during the Hunger Winter

tubes. People rode bicycles without tires, using wooden slat "tires," or stopped riding.

Clothing was so run-down and shabby that most people in Holland resembled tramps. Shoe heels were worn off, and parents cut the toes off children's shoes to accommodate growing feet. People added layers of worn-out clothing, even rags, to keep warm during cold days. To get more wear from their clothing, they applied patches and mended what they could, turning old clothing inside out if possible. Tailors and cobblers had more work than they could handle, but fixing old items cost more than what they had once cost new. Hats, stockings, and coats were luxuries.

During the 1944-1945 winter, there was hardly any coal, gas, or electricity. Amsterdammers struggled through the winter months to stay warm, burning whole streets of trees, furniture, and any other wood they could find. Vacant homes were ransacked for floorboards and other wood items. For light, people relied upon candles.

The lack of food that same winter reached a crisis point and was known as the "Hunger Winter." The Nazis were furious that the Dutch would not cooperate and, instead, were sabotaging German military operations. They cut off food shipments by rail to towns and cities throughout Holland. When winter came, barges could not get down the frozen rivers into Amsterdam, either.

Now, thousands of women and children and the few remaining men searched the Dutch countryside for food. They often had to trade valued possessions in order to eat. According to Henk Aben, "You changed against paintings, stamps, cigarettes, or wedding rings."[10] Marion Pritchard recalls, "I made the trip with my bicycle (by this time without tires), took my flute and some of the family silver, and was able to buy what seemed like a wonderful supply of food. The Germans were constantly patrolling the roads...."[11]

During the *hongertochts*—hunger walks—people with baby carriages and pushcarts trudged for hours in freezing weather to reach a farm. Often, they got only some flour, a few potatoes and carrots, or some kale, even after searching for a week or more. Berend Beins assumed responsibility for getting food needed by former co-workers whose jobs and ration coupons had been taken by Nazis. While carrying food, he fooled Nazi patrols by hanging oil cans and blueprints on his bicycle without tires. He says, "People who had spotted Nazi patrols helped by calling out, 'Take that road today; it's better.'"[12] Relatives and friends of farmers might get milk, butter, or meat.

Those who could not get enough food lined up at public kitchens for broth made of sugar beets, potatoes, or carrots. At their peak, Amsterdam's public kitchens served 300,000 people. The Swiss and Swedish Red Cross sent food, but people got only about 500 calories a day during that harsh winter. Many stayed alive by eating tulip bulbs. About 400 Dutch died of starvation every day during the Hunger Winter.

Weak, hungry, and frightened, people struggled from day to day. Yet they managed to have some pleasant times amid the hardships. Families, traditionally close-knit in Holland, had become used to spending more time together because of the curfews and lack of outside activities. Henk Aben remembers that last winter:

> No gas, no electricity, no water. Problems everywhere. But many will remember the long, long nights with just one candle, doing games or listening to the jammed BBC or Radio Orange in London. Strange enough, those evenings were considered *gezellig* [cozy]. Of course because of the togetherness, the shared last slice of bread.[13]

The trees around Amsterdam were cut down for fuel during the harsh winter.

Surviving under stress and living with bare essentials gave many people a sense of inner strength.

There was also a sense of unity as people faced their Nazi oppressors together. People read more books, often selecting ones that related past struggles, and they formed classes and discussion groups. Resistance members got satisfaction from outwitting the Nazis and saving people in hiding.

Still, the Hunger Winter and the continuing Nazi persecution began to seem like an endless nightmare. Now Dutch girls and women were also being picked up for forced labor. During the early months of 1945, they were taken off the streets by soldiers pointing submachine guns at them, who took them to work in German camps, military hospitals, and kitchens.

By 1945, the Nazis had deported most of the 140,000 Jews who lived in Holland before the war. They had been sent to death camps, including Mauthausen, Auschwitz, Theresienstadt, and Bergen-Belsen. Before the war ended, 110,000 Dutch Jews were dead. Writing of this tragedy, Jacob Presser calls it "the story of murder—murder on a scale never known before, with malice aforethought and in cold blood."[14]

As 1945 began, the people of Amsterdam, listening closely to their radios, heard that Allied forces were steadily defeating the Germans and had already liberated part of Holland. Yet around them, people were starving. The dead were so numerous that bodies were buried in cardboard boxes or paper sacks. From London, Queen Wilhelmina expressed alarm, saying that Holland might be a nation of corpses when freedom finally came. In April, with all electric power gone and no fuel even for public kitchens, Amsterdammers continued their desperate struggle to survive.

Dutch citizens wave an American flag to welcome a U.S. plane.

★★★★★★★★★

6

REBUILDING A STRICKEN NATION

Early in 1945, the people of Amsterdam and other occupied areas waited wearily for Allied forces to arrive. Germany had met with defeat in Russia, and Berlin and other German cities had been destroyed by Allied planes. The BBC and underground newspapers had reported the fall of Italy's Fascist government and the liberation of Hungary, France, and the Dutch province of Limburg by American and British troops. At the end of 1944, Allied troops had entered Germany itself.

Miep Gies wrote that during the spring of 1945, there was "a sickly smell of endlessly boiling tulip bulbs or pulpy sugar beets, or badly washed clothing hanging to dry, or bodies wrapped too long in ragged clothes."[1] By then, she and her husband no longer had a

An Allied plane makes a food drop over Amsterdam.

radio. Chronically hungry, they imagined the good food they would eat someday. They spent some of their time copying recipes from cookbooks by the light of a string they had dipped in oil and floated in a glass of water.

As Germany's defeat seemed certain, German and Dutch Nazis began fleeing Holland. The Germans were no longer fit and well-dressed as they had been five years before when they arrived in Amsterdam. They were thin, with shabby clothing, more like the people they had victimized. Those who fled took any money and property they could find and carry.

Leesha Rose, a member of the Dutch underground, wrote that German soldiers began offering the resistance weapons, motorbikes, and other supplies in exchange for places to hide until the war ended. It was ironic that the men who had persecuted her fellow Jews and sent her family to concentration camps were now asking for help in exchange for guns.[2]

April 29, 1945, was an unforgettable day in Holland. Allied planes began dropping food packages into the country. Walter Maass saw the squadrons of low-flying Allied bombers overhead:

> The radio had announced that relief planes would be coming....Who had ever heard of planes dropping food parcels in territory occupied by the enemy? The Germans would never permit it. But now it had come true....The whole population stood on the streets waving and shouting. Many were crying. And one excited exclamation was heard again and again, "Now we shall soon be free."[3]

Maass writes that people:

> stood on their roofs and balconies and cheered the Allied planes. For weeks people had lived on two slices of bread per day and a few frost-spoilt potatoes and vegetables....Thousands had already greeted the British aviators with Dutch flags. But the Green Police kept riding with helmets and machine guns through the streets....[4]

Leesha Rose found that the crates contained:

> cheese, meat, potatoes, flour, vegetables, tea, chocolate, and sugar....Our gratefulness was beyond words. We recognized the American Fortresses and greeted them like welcome friends....We were finally being linked up with the living world outside the borders of the Netherlands.[5]

The news came that Adolf Hitler had committed suicide on April 30. Then, on May 4, five gruesome years of war finally ended. The Germans surrendered unconditionally to Allied Field Marshal Bernard Montgomery. On May 5, the papers freeing the western Netherlands were formally signed.

There was little electricity, so few radios were operating that day. Miep Gies was cooking carrots and potatoes over a fire made of wood chips when her husband, Henk, ran in with the news: "The Germans have capitulated. The war is over!"[6]

Newspapers announced: THE BEST NEWS OF THIS WAR and NETHERLANDS SHALL RISE AGAIN!!!!! People ignored the eight o'clock curfew and crowded the streets of Amsterdam to celebrate. They lit bonfires, and people released flocks of pigeons, birds which had been banned during the Occupation to prevent them from being used as messenger pigeons. People laughed, sang, danced, and embraced each other.

The end of five years of war: citizens of Amsterdam welcome victorious Allied troops into the city.

May 8 was the official Victory Day in Holland. Canadian and other Allied troops in Amsterdam were greeted with flowers, kisses, and the waving of the Dutch flag. Leesha Rose said, "Dutch boys and girls hung on their tanks....They waved and cheered and sang...the 'Wilhemus.'"[7] Rose was especially proud to see soldiers from the Jewish Brigade from Palestine, which had fought with the British 8th Army.

The Liberation brought relief and the end of Nazi brutality in Holland. But the nation and its people had been devastated physically, emotionally, and economically. Historian Walter Maass, himself a survivor, described the Dutch as "tired, hungry, and some-

A crowd celebrates on Victory Day.

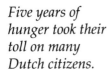
Five years of hunger took their toll on many Dutch citizens.

what bewildered—[like] a patient who leaves the hospital after a long and painful illness."[8]

The Dutch faced a difficult period of rebuilding the country. One immediate problem was the lack of enough housing. About 25% of the people in Europe needed housing. Air raids, shellfire, and street fighting had caused heavy damage. The Germans had destroyed buildings in Holland from the onset of the Occupation and during their retreat. They had opened dykes and sluices, flooding acres of land in order to keep out the Allies. All this land had to be drained before it was suitable for building or farming.

The U.S. government later implemented a form of aid called the European Recovery Program, or Marshall Plan, which provided cement, steel, and other materials needed for new housing. In the meantime, the people of Amsterdam and other Dutch communities rebuilt burned-out masonry houses and used whatever shelter they could find, including abandoned windmills.

Holland was still plagued by hunger and disease. There was not enough fertilizer, labor, machinery, seed, or livestock to provide crops and other foods needed in the near future. Food was more plentiful than it had been during the war, but rationing continued. The food supply did not approach prewar levels until 1950. After the war, the Red Cross and United States sent relief packages containing canned foods, soap, clothing, blankets, and other goods.

Many Dutch teenagers took part in the postwar work. Jan Jonkheer and his friend Piet, who were freed from prison during the Liberation, joined other Dutch teenagers who helped to rebuild the country. Teenagers worked in hospitals and rest homes, aiding returning soldiers and civilians. They built shelters, drained land, and worked on farms and in the dairy industry.

For Jews who had hidden or been deported and survived, there were profound adjustments. Ida Vos remembers:

> It is May 1945, and I am allowed to go outside again. American and Canadian soldiers have come to chase the Germans away. I may go to school again. I am 13 years old and I am only in the fifth grade....I may go swimming again. I may go to the library, I may sit on a bench again. I may spend the night away from home.[9]

Yet the war had brought lasting pain for Ida and her family:

> I want to visit my grandparents, but I can't. I can't visit my cousins Marga and Meintje, either, for they are all dead. They were killed because they were Jews....Can you imagine how it feels when you find out that people you love are dead, all of a sudden?[10]

After being freed from the Bergen-Belsen camp, Dr. and Mrs. Werner Weinberg had to wait two months before they could get back to Holland to find their daughter, Susie. Now four years old, Susie had been hidden by a Dutch couple with three children. Dr. Weinberg later wrote, "It took three more weeks before we were able to arrange for a truck ride to Amsterdam. We found the new address [where the Red Cross had said Susie was staying]. Outside, little children were playing. Was Susie among them?"[11] Overjoyed, the Weinbergs found their daughter and embraced her, after a two-year separation.

While the war's end meant happy reunions for many families, other people's lives had been shattered. Some people knew their loved ones had died; others had to search for missing relatives and friends. Letters from the Red Cross told people if and when family members would arrive home. The railroads had been damaged, so newly freed political prisoners, forced laborers, and concentration camp survivors returned slowly.

Walter Maass described the "small groups of pale, sick, emaciated people"[12] who arrived by train. Bone-thin survivors wore ill-fitting clothing donated by the Red Cross. Many women wore scarves to hide their heads, which had been shaved by the Nazis. Concentration camp victims had blue numbers tattooed on their arms, a lasting reminder that they had been considered numbers, not people, by their tormentors.

As people returned, the Dutch learned the extent of the brutalities committed by Nazis at camps where about 11 million people—6 million of them Jewish—had died. More than 100,000 Dutch Jews had died, in addition to the thousands of Dutch civilians who had died of starvation, illness, or military violence. During World War II, 50 million people—more than in any other war—died. About 17 million were military casualties; the remainder were civilians.

During the summer of 1945, the residents of Amsterdam began to rebuild their lives with the help of Allied relief groups.

Some loved ones did not return. Miep Gies writes of the day on which Otto Frank, at work in his office, received a letter from the Red Cross telling him the fate of his daughters. Gies said that his voice was totally crushed as he told her, "Miep, Margot and Anne are not coming back."[13] The two girls had died of typhus in the squalid Bergen-Belsen camp in March 1945, just two months before the Liberation. His family dead, Otto Frank lived with Miep and Henk Gies for the next seven years.

Throughout Europe, there were millions of refugees, called "displaced persons," who had no place to go. Some people had lost their jobs, families, homes, and possessions. Many Jews had such terrible memories that they could not bear to stay in Europe. They emigrated to other places, including Palestine, where Jews worked to develop a recognized Jewish homeland.

Such massive losses and changes required enormous adjustments. Historian Adriaan Barnouw explained,

> When daily life is lived in constant anticipation of something dreadful to happen, the minutes creep by at a snail's pace....People aged quickly in those years that were centuries. The young became middle-aged under the impact of hard, incredibly cruel experience, and children were grown up before they had known youth.[14]

After the Liberation, the Dutch government, like others in Europe, arrested persons suspected of treason or collaboration with the Nazis, then conducted trials for war criminals. Nearly 200,000 suspects were detained, of whom 66,000 were convicted.

The Allied countries considered how to deal with the high-ranking Nazis most responsible for the death and destruction that occurred during the war. An international court was convened in November 1946, in Nuremburg, Germany. Twenty-four Nazi officials were charged with mass murder, mistreatment of prisoners of war, deliberate crimes against racial and religious groups, and deportation of thousands of people to slave labor. Among those men was Arthur Seyss-Inquart, who had directed Nazi activities in the Netherlands. Along with the others, Seyss-Inquart was convicted of war crimes and crimes against humanity. He and eleven other men were hanged to death on October 16, 1946.

At 8:00 P.M., on May 4 every year, the traffic in Amsterdam pulls to the side of the road, and radio and television programs are interrupted. People stop whatever they are doing and pause to remember the war dead and to pray for peace. This is the Dutch Memorial Day, a public holiday commemorating the end of World War II. Funeral music is played, followed by the Dutch national anthem.

At the Dam Square is the National Monument, dedicated as a war memorial in 1956. Members of the Dutch royal family lay a wreath here each year. Many people mark the day by going to church or putting flowers on the places where Dutch Resistance fighters were killed. On the following day, there are parades and festivals, a joyous celebration of Liberation Day.

During the stressful Occupation, children often lived without one or both parents and suffered from many other hardships. They had to keep important secrets when the family was hiding hunted people. Many worked in the resistance. In recognition of their contributions, in 1950, Princess Margriet and her mother, Queen Juliana, dedicated a statue "to the courage of Dutch Youth through the ages." The brave Amsterdammers who led the 1941 strike are remembered on February 25 each year when citizens gather around the Statue of the Dockworker in their honor.

People who survived the Occupation have lasting memories.

The famous film actress Audrey Hepburn lived in Holland from age 11 to 16 during those years. She once said:

> The war left me with a deep knowledge of human suffering which I expect many other young people never know about. The things I saw during the occupation made me very realistic about life, and I've been that way ever since....I came out of the war thankful to be alive, aware that human relationships are the most important thing of all, far more than wealth, food, luxury, careers, or anything you can mention.[15]

Along with the rest of Holland, Amsterdam survived the grim war years. Today, the people again live peaceful lives. Dutch industries have been rebuilt, and the dairy and bulb businesses are important sources of export income. Again, the city's port thrives with ships from countries around the world.

Amsterdam, along with Paris, London, and Rome, is one of the most visited capital cities in Europe. Besides the art museums, elegant restaurants, canals, and flower stalls, one sees reminders of war: the Dockworker Statue, the National Monument, and the Anne Frank House, now a famous museum. The character of Amsterdam and its people was summarized by the late Queen Wilhelmina in a motto she presented to the city:

HEROIC, RESOLUTE, MERCIFUL

The Statue of the Dockworker, erected in memory of those who took part in the 1941 strike.

SOURCE NOTES

∗ ∗ ∗

CHAPTER
ONE

1. Fradin, Dennis B., *The Netherlands* (Chicago: Children's Press, 1983), 11.
2. Geoffrey Cotterell, *Amsterdam: The Life of a City* (Boston: Little Brown, 1972), frontispiece.
3. Ibid., 265.
4. Miep Gies (with Alison Leslie Gold), *Anne Frank Remembered: The Story of the Woman Who Helped to Hide the Frank Family* (New York: Simon and Schuster, 1987), 40.
5. Jan Jonkheer, "The SS5: Pages from Jan's Diary," in Lore Cowan, ed. *Children of the Resistance* (New York: Meredith Press, 1969), 106.
6. Ibid., 106-107.

CHAPTER
TWO

1. Gies, 53.
2. Jonkheer, 107.
3. Walter B. Maass, *The Netherlands at War: 1940-1945* (New York: Abelard-Schuman, 1970), 32.
4. Corrie ten Boom, with John and Elizabeth Sherrill, *The Hiding Place* (Boston: G.K. Hall, 1973), 117.
5. Dirk van der Heide [pseud.] *My Sister and I: The Story of a Dutch Boy Refugee* (New York: Harcourt, 1941) quoted in Desmond Flower and James Reeves, eds., *The Taste of Courage: The War, 1939-1945* (New York: Harper, 1960), 52-53.
6. van der Heide, 50.
7. Jonkheer, 107-108.
8. van der Heide, 54-55.
9. Maass, 39.
10. Ibid., 41.
11. Leesha Rose. *The Tulips Are Red* (New York: A.S. Barnes and Co., 1978), 18-19.
12. Ibid., 19.
13. Ibid., 18.
14. Gies, 55.
15. Rose, 16-17.
16. Ida Vos, *Hide and Seek* [published in Holland as *Wie Niet Weg is Wordt Gezien*. 1981, by Uitgeverij Leopold] (New York: Houghton Mifflin, 1991), vii.

1. Adriaan J. Barnouw, *The Pageant of Netherlands History* (New York: Longmans Green and Co., 1952), 332.
2. Interview with the author: July 21, 1991.
3. Norman Rich, *Hitler's War Aims: The Establishment of the New Order* (New York: W.W. Norton, 1973), 143.
4. Jonkheer, 108.
5. Jonkheer, 110-111.
6. Louis de Jong, *The Lion Rampant: The Story of Holland's Resistance to the Nazis* trans. from the Dutch by Joseph W.F. Stoppelman. (New York: Querido, 1945), 298.
7. De Jong, 52.
8. Interview with the author: July 21, 1991.
9. Milton Meltzer, *Rescue: The Story of How Gentiles Saved Jews During the Holocaust* (New York: Harper and Row, 1988), 6.
10. Quoted in Carol Rittner and Sondra Meyers, eds. *The Courage to Care: Rescuers of Jews During the Holocaust* (New York: New York University Press, 1986), 28.
11. Barnouw, 332.
12. Rich, 160.
13. Rose, 29.
14. De Jong, 188.
15. Ibid., 193.
16. Rose, 42-43.
17. Ibid., 43.

CHAPTER THREE

1. De Jong, 74.
2. Interview with the author: July 21, 1991.
3. Gies, 71.
4. Vos, vii.
5. De Jong, 190.
6. Ibid.
7. Ibid., 191.
8. Quoted in Rittner and Meyers, 24.
9. Jonkheer, 114.
10. Interview with the author: July 21, 1991.
11. Kiryl Sosnowski, *The Tragedy of Children Under Nazi Rule*, trans. from the Polish: *Dziecko w systemie hitlerowskim* (New York: Howard Fertig, Inc., 1983), 106.
12. Letter to the author: February 2, 1991.

CHAPTER FOUR

13. Deborah Dwórk, *Children With a Star: Jewish Youth in Nazi Europe* (New Haven: Yale University Press, 1991), 25.
14. Telephone interview with the author: June 5, 1991.
15. Dwork, 26.
16. Philip Friedman, *Their Brothers' Keepers: The Christian Heroes and Heroines Who Helped the Oppressed Escape Nazi Terror* (New York: Holocaust Library, 1978), 64-65.
17. Quoted in Rittner and Meyers, 29.
18. Ibid., 27.
19. Dwork, 37.
20. Ibid., 41.
21. Anne Frank, *Anne Frank: The Diary of a Young Girl* (trans. from the Dutch, *Het Achterhuis—The Annex*—by B. M. Mooyaart), (Garden City, N.Y.: Doubleday, 1952), 13.
22. Ibid., 19.
23. Dwork, 73.
24. Werner Warmbrunn, *The Dutch Under German Occupation: 1940-1945* (Stanford, Calif.: Stanford University Press, 1963), 172-173.
25. De Jong, 192.

CHAPTER
FIVE

1. Interview with the author: July 21, 1991.
2. De Jong, 96.
3. Ibid., 98.
4. Ina B. Friedman, *Escape or Die* (Reading, Mass.: Addison-Wesley, 1982), 72-78.
5. Ina B. Friedman, *The Other Victims: First-Person Stories of Non-Jews Persecuted by the Nazis* (Boston: Houghton Mifflin, 1990), 169-170.
6. Ibid.
7. Dwork, 75.
8. Ibid.
9. Frank, 156.
10. Letter to the author: February 2, 1991.
11. Quoted in Rittner and Meyers, 32.
12. Interview with the author: July 21, 1991.
13. Letter to the author: February 2, 1991.
14. Jacob Presser, *The Destruction of the Dutch Jews* (New York: Dutton, 1969), 1.

1. Gies, 192.
2. Rose, 244-245.
3. Maass, 239-240.
4. Ibid., 241.
5. Rose, 251.
6. Gies, 194.
7. Rose, 267.
8. Maass, 247.
9. Vos, viii-ix.
10. Ibid., ix.
11. Werner Weinberg, "A Dutch Couple," *The Christian Century*, June 22-29, 1983, 614.
12. Maass, 247.
13. Gies, 204.
14. Barnouw, 327.
15. Ian Woodward, *Audrey Hepburn* (New York: St. Martin's Press, 1984), 39.

CHAPTER
SIX

FURTHER READING

* * *

Abells, Chana Byers. *The Children We Remember*. New York: Greenwillow, 1986.

Druks, Herbert. *Jewish Resistance During the Holocaust*. New York: Irvington Publishers, 1983.

Friedman, Philip. *Their Brothers' Keepers: The Christian Heroes and Heroines Who Helped the Oppressed Escape Nazi Terror*. New York: Holocaust Library, 1978.

Gilbert, Martin. *The Fate of the Jews in Nazi Europe*. New York: Mayflower, 1979.

Hoffman, Ann. *The Dutch: How They Live and Work*. New York: Praeger, 1973.

Keegan, John. *The Second World War*. New York: Viking, 1989.

Lindwer, Willy. trans. Alison Meersschaert. *The Last Seven Months of Anne Frank*. New York: Pantheon, 1991.

Meltzer, Milton. *Never to Forget: The Jews of the Holocaust*. New York: Harper and Row, 1976.

———. *Rescue: The Story of How Gentiles Saved Jews During the Holocaust*. New York: Harper and Row, 1988.

Messenger, Charles. *The Second World War*. New York: Franklin Watts, 1987.

Reiss, Johanna. *The Upstairs Room*. New York: Bantam, 1980.

Rossiter, Margaret. *Women in the Resistance*. New York: Praeger, 1986.

Savage, Katherine. *The Story of the Second World War*. New York: Henry Z. Walck, Inc., 1958.

Stadtler, Bea. *The Holocaust: A History of Courage and Resistance*. New York: Behrman House, 1973.

Stein, Andre. *Quiet Heroes: True Stories of the Rescue of Jews by Christians in Nazi-Occupied Holland*. Toronto: Lester & Orpen Dennys, 1988.

Yoors, Jan. *Crossing: A Journal of Survival and Resistance in Nazi Europe*. New York: Simon and Schuster, 1963.

INDEX

* * *